THE SECRET OF HAPPY ALONE

SARATH KUMAR S

ISBN 979-888530866-3

Contents

Preface

Do you remember when you were younger–maybe 12 or 13–and your parents would go out to run errands or something and leave you home alone?

If you're like me, the second you heard that door shut and you had the house to yourself, you felt this incredible sense of unprecedented freedom to do whatever you wanted for the next few hours–and it was absolutely wonderful.

Building a good relationship with yourself is a worthy investment. Being alone isn't the same as being lonely.Before getting into the ins of being happy alone, it's important to understand that being alone doesn't have to mean you're lonely.This book is aimed at helping you get the ball rolling.They might not transform your life overnight, but they can help you get more comfortable with being alone.Some of them may be exactly what you needed to hear. Others may not make sense for you.Use them as stepping-stones.Add to them and shape them along the way to suit your own lifestyle and personality.

MAKE THE MOST OF "ME TIME."

CHAPTER ONE

Stop Comparisons

Personality begins where comparison leaves off. Be unique. Be memorable. Be confident. Be proud. Job title, income, grades, house, and Facebook likes—the number of categories in which we can compare ourselves to others are infinite. So is the number of people we can compare ourselves to.Comparison is generally the fast track to unhappiness. It's a recipe for misery. All it does is keeping you focused on what you don't like about yourself and your life.

This is easier said than done, but try to avoid comparing your social life to anyone else's. It's not the number of friends you have or the frequency of your social outings that matters. It's what works for you.

Remember, you really have no way of knowing if someone with a bunch of friends and a stuffed social calendar is actually happy.

CHAPTER TWO

Take Yourself on a Date

They might sound cliche, but self-dates can be a powerful tool for learning how to be happy alone.

Not sure what to do? Imagine you're trying to impress an actual date and show them a good time. Where would you take them? What would you want them to see or experience?

Now, take yourself on that date. It might feel a bit odd at first, but chances are, you'll see at least a few other folks dining solo or purchasing a movie ticket for one.

If money's an issue, you don't have to go big. But also remember it's a lot cheaper to pay for one than it is for two.

Still sounds too daunting? Start small by sitting in a coffee shop for just 10 minutes. Be observant and soak in your surroundings. Once you're comfortable with that, going out alone won't seem so unusual anymore.

CHAPTER THREE

Spend Time with Nature

Yes, another cliche. But seriously, get outside. Lounge in the backyard, take a walk in the park, or hang out by the water. Absorb the sights, sounds, and smells of nature. Feel the breeze on your face.

Researches shows that 30 minutes or more a week spent in nature or green space can improve symptoms of depression and lower blood pressure.Your green space could be anything from your neighborhood park, your own backyard, or a rooftop garden — anywhere you can appreciate some nature and fresh air.

CHAPTER FOUR

Find a Creative Outlet

What have you always dreamed of doing, but have put off? Don't worry if you're not good at it. The point is to try something new and different, to take a step outside your comfort zone.

Take on a home improvement project. Learn to play an instrument, paint a landscape, or write a short story or poem. Do it on your own or enroll in a class. Give yourself ample time to see if it's worth pursuing.

If you don't like it, you can at least cross it off your list and move on to something else.

CHAPTER FIVE

Go to a Movie Alone

Get used to doing things alone that society says is made for two. Go to a movie by yourself and enjoy the picture. Have a great dinner out all by yourself. Take yourself on dates, and learn to treat yourself well.

This will be awkward at first. If you're used to going out with others, you'll wonder what you should do with yourself while you're alone. Don't try to hide from the discomfort. Accept it. And then laugh about it because, really, who the hell decided that you weren't supposed to do these things alone?

Besides, to truly enjoy these things with others, you have to learn to enjoy them alone first.

CHAPTER SIX

Nurture Relationships

As you become more comfortable being alone, you might find yourself spending less time socializing. There's nothing wrong with that, but close social connections are still important.

Arrange to visit with someone in your family, a friend, or go hang out with the team after work. Call someone you haven't heard from in a long time and have a meaningful conversation.

Take Care of your Health

Mental health can affect physical health and vice versa. Taking care of your physical health may help boost your overall happiness. Plus, it's a good way to foster a good relationship with yourself.

Exercise isn't just for your body. Regular exercise can help to reduce stress, feelings of anxiety, and symptoms of depression while boosting self-esteem and happiness.

Even a small amount of physical activity can make a difference. You don't have to train for a triathlon or scale a cliff — unless that's what makes you happy, of course.

Make eating a balanced diet, exercising regularly, and getting plenty of sleep part of what you do with your alone time. Be sure to get an annual physical, and see your doctor to manage any preexisting health conditions.

Trust Yourself

Don't ask for advice unless you truly need it. Instead, ask yourself for advice. If you knew the answer to the problem that you have, what would it be?

That's your answer. The more time you spend asking yourself for advice, the less you start to need input from others. When you trust yourself to solve problems, you become a much stronger and more confident person, and you take on challenges that you wouldn't have felt capable of before.

Learn to be an Observer

If you aren't able to take interest in something, it says more about you than whatever it is you find uninteresting.

To truly enjoy being alone, learn to look at ordinary situations in new and unfamiliar ways. Go to the park and watch people play with their children or their dogs. Go to the grocery store and watch how people shop for their groceries.

Everywhere you go, make an effort to understand the other people around you. Learning how people operate when they think no one is watching will make you feel more connected to them.

CHAPTER TEN

Appreciate the Silence

The world is a busy place and, unless you take a moment to step away from it once in a while, it's easy to forget how nice it is to simply sit alone and enjoy your own company.

Take a moment and sit quietly in a dark room. Listen to everything that is not happening around you. You can learn a lot about yourself in the moments when you're least occupied—the times when there is nothing to distract you from the thoughts and feelings you deny yourself during your busy days.

CHAPTER ELEVEN

Cherish Interactions

Most people have to experience some type of tragedy before they begin to understand just how brief our time here is. You get but a few short trips around the sun, and then it's over.

Time alone is important. Time alone is beautiful. But so is time spent with others.

There is no such thing as a boring person. There is no such thing as a boring situation. If you're ever bored, it's because you're not paying attention. This is a problem with you, not with your surroundings.

Take an interest in every person that comes into your life, even if for only a second. Listen closely to what they say. Watch carefully what they do. Try to understand them as a person. You'll be better for it.

CHAPTER TWELVE

Volunteer your Time

If you're a hermit when you're alone, find others that you can be alone around. A great way to do this—and to contribute something positive to the world—is to volunteer your time to a cause you believe in.

Being alone and happy doesn't mean sequestering yourself from the world. It means being confident enough to know that you can surround yourself with people, but not depend on them for your own happiness.

And one good way to get started is to surround yourself with good people—the kind you'll find when you give your time to a cause that's important to you.

CHAPTER THIRTEEN

Make Plans for the Future

It's almost impossible to feel good about your life if you don't have some type of direction for it. When you meet someone, it's usually quite easy to see if they have a handle on their life and are happy, or if they're wandering without aim, looking for something to pursue.

The purpose for your life doesn't need to be complex or earth shattering. It doesn't have to be big or overwhelming. It only needs to be present. Once it's there, it gets much easier to make plans you can take action on.

Pursue these plans immediately. Don't put them off. Don't wait for the perfect opportunity. Perfect never comes, and the longer you wait, the harder it is to get started.

Maybe you want to travel the world and understand different cultures. Maybe you want to build a massive stamp collection. It doesn't matter what it is—pick something you enjoy and go after it.

When you do this, two things happen. First, you gain a sense of confidence in yourself because you see that you're capable of living on your own terms. Second, this confidence brings new and interesting people into your life.

Being alone can be beautiful, but if you want to add people to your life, finding a purpose for your existence is the fastest way to do it.

CHAPTER FOURTEEN

Acknowledge the Unhappy Moments

A positive attitude is generally a good thing, but bad things happen to everyone. It's just part of life.

If you get some bad news, make a mistake, or just feel like you're in a funk, don't try to pretend you're happy.

Acknowledge the feeling of unhappiness, letting yourself experience it for a moment. Then, shift your focus toward what made you feel this way and what it might take to recover.

Would a deep breathing exercise help? A long walk outside? Talking it over with someone?

Let the moment pass and take care of yourself. Remember, no one's happy all the time.

CHAPTER FIFTEEN

Create, Create, Create

To create is one of the most important things you can do in your life. To create among a sea of people (or even just one person) vying for your attention is one of the most difficult things in life.

When you're alone, the only one stopping you from creating the art, the work, that you're capable of is yourself. All excuses are gone. When you're alone, you can lose yourself in your work. When you lose yourself in your work, you can be sure that you're creating something truly meaningful.

Your other option is to ignore that call to create and, instead, look for temporary comfort in things and people who will eventually leave you unfulfilled. Make use of your loneliness.

MAKE THE MOST OF "ME TIME."